LEADERS OF
ANCIENT EGYPT

RAMESES II   Pharaoh of the
New Kingdom

LEADERS OF
ANCIENT EGYPT

RAMESES II

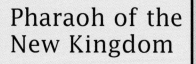

Pharaoh of the New Kingdom

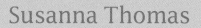

Susanna Thomas

the rosen publishing group's
rosen
central

For Joseph and Fred Thomas

Published in 2003 by The Rosen Publishing Group, Inc.
29 East 21st Street, New York, NY 10010

First Edition

Library of Congress Cataloging-in-Publication Data

Thomas, Susanna.
Rameses II: pharaoh of the new kingdom / Susanna
Thomas.— 1st ed.
    p. cm.—(Leaders of ancient Egypt)
Includes bibliographical references and index.
Summary: Examines the life and times of the man who ruled Egypt from 1279 to 1213 B.C., in the period when that kingdom was at its most powerful, and who built more monuments throughout Egypt than any other pharaoh.
ISBN 0–8239–3597–3 (library binding)
1. Ramses II, King of Egypt—Juvenile literature. 2. Egypt—History—Nineteenth dynasty, ca. 1320–1200 B.C.—Juvenile literature. 3. Pharaohs—Biography—Juvenile literature.
[1. Ramses II, King of Egypt. 2. Kings, queens, rulers, etc. 3. Egypt—Civilization—To 332 B.C.] I. Title. II. Series.
DT88 .T46 2002
932'.014'092—dc21

2001006635

Manufactured in the United States of America

Contents

ANCIENT EGYPT

CANAAN

MEDITERRANEAN SEA

LIBYA

• Alexandria

Nile Delta

LOWER EGYPT

• Avaris

• Heliopolis

• Cairo

Giza •

Memphis •
Saqqara •

Dashur •

Meidum •

FAIYUM

SINAI

• el-Amarna

EASTERN DESERT

UPPER EGYPT

WESTERN DESERT

RED SEA

Abydos •

• Dendera

• Thebes

• Karnak
• Luxor

River Nile

• Elephantine
• Aswan

Abu Simbel •

NUBIA

INTRODUCTION

Rameses II was the third king of the Nineteenth Dynasty. He reigned between 1279 and 1213 BC in the middle of a period known as the New Kingdom, when Egypt was at its most powerful. The country prospered under him and experienced an era of both internal and external stability. By the end of his sixty-six-year-long reign, his name was famous throughout the ancient world.

Rameses built more monuments throughout the whole of Egypt and Nubia (modern-day Sudan) than any other pharaoh, and also took the buildings and statues of previous pharaohs and renamed them as if he had made them himself. By the end of his reign, colossal statues of the king were worshiped in all the main cities of Egypt. He had many wives and nearly a hundred children,

A statue of Rameses II in the colonnaded court of his temple at Luxor, Egypt.

some of whom are known today through inscriptions and illustrations, as well as through the discovery of their tombs.

One of Rameses' primary goals was to be known and remembered as a great warrior. The image of the brave fighter single-handedly defending his kingdom was one that Rameses called up even in his old age, and the walls of his temples are covered with paintings of successful military campaigns. These paintings show the king leading his troops into battle and defeating the enemy in personal combat.

Rameses was a military leader who courageously fought invading armies and saved Egypt from her enemies. This is his story, a story based on Egyptian records, and it offers a very different portrait of Rameses II from the one readers may be familiar with from the Old Testament. Egyptian records make no mention of the oppression of the Hebrews, the plagues, the Exodus, the pillar of fire, or the pharaoh's army drowned in the Red Sea. Here instead is a portrait of a dynamic leader who made his nation both stable and prosperous.

A wall painting of Rameses I, grandfather of Rameses II, taken from the tomb of Horemheb in the Valley of the Kings at Thebes.

THE RAMESES DYNASTY

Rameses' grandfather, Rameses I, had been a general and a *vizier* (a secretary of state), under Horemheb, the last king of the Eighteenth Dynasty of ancient Egypt. He held the title Deputy of the King of Upper and Lower Egypt, as had his friend Horemheb before him, and the transition of power seems to have been a peaceful one.

Horemheb didn't have any children, and Rameses must have seemed the safest and most sensible choice to be the next pharaoh of Egypt. His importance was reflected in the list of jobs he performed for Horemheb: Chief of Archers, Chief of Seals, Superintendent of Horses, King's Charioteer, Commander of the Army of the Ruler of Two Lands, High Priest of all the Gods, Superintendent of the Mouths of the Nile, and Hereditary Prince of the Entire Land.

A wall carving depicting the symbolic union of Upper and Lower Egypt.

Horemheb himself had not inherited the throne in the normal way—that is, by assuming it upon his father's death. He had been a successful general when his predecessor, King Ay, who also had no children of his own, appointed him to be the next pharaoh. The appointment of both these kings shows how important military positions were at this time. When Horemheb was in his sixties and Rameses I was in his fifties, Rameses was appointed as the heir. Rameses' eldest son, Seti, was already an adult by this time, and was a soldier who was married to Tuya, who also came from a military family. They had at least two daughters as well as a son, also called Rameses. This was an additional factor in Horemheb's decision to make Rameses I the successor. Rameses not only had sons but grandsons to act as heirs to the throne and to carry on the new dynasty.

Horemheb died in 1295 BC, and the first royal act of Rameses I was to oversee his secret burial rites in the Valley of the Kings on the west bank of the Nile at Luxor. At the same time, Rameses began preparations for his own tomb to be built near that of his friend Horemheb in the Valley of the Kings, as well as a memorial temple on the flood plain below the valley where ritual offerings could be made after he died.

While still at Luxor, Rameses decided to make his mark as the new ruler. The most important god in Egypt during the New Kingdom was Amen-Re, and the main center in the country for worshipping this god was at the Karnak Temple in Luxor. Rameses I and his son Seti planned to build a fabulous addition to this temple by adding a huge hall of enormous columns, called a hypostyle hall, in between the two existing pylon gateways. He also decided that the walls of the two gateways, as well as the ceilings and columns of the hall, should be redecorated with pictures of temple rituals and the names of Rameses and Seti.

After beginning these different building projects, Rameses I and Seti then sailed north down the Nile back to the capital at Memphis (near modern Cairo). Seti was sent back to the army, where he trained troops, and he also led a small military expedition into Canaan (modern Israel). Toward the end of the Eighteenth Dynasty, many of Egypt's territories in the Near East—Israel, Jordan, Lebanon, and Syria—had been lost, and one of Seti's ambitions was to restore Egypt's Syrian empire. Rameses also sent fresh supplies to a fortress at the other end of his empire in Nubia (modern Sudan) to reassure the troops posted there that they were not forgotten.

Detail of the falcon-headed god Horus, from a painting in the tomb of Horemheb, the last king of the Eighteenth Dynasty.

Unlike the kings of the Eighteenth Dynasty, whose families originally came from Luxor, Rameses' family came from the northeast corner of the Nile Delta. Rameses I had a holiday house near Avaris where the Hyksos kings of the Second Intermediate Period had lived. Egyptians usually felt particular loyalty to the town or area where they were born, and it is likely that Rameses planned to celebrate being made pharaoh by building special temples or palaces in this region. However, after about only one year in office, Rameses I fell ill. He appointed his son Seti as co-regent, and after only one year and four months of ruling Egypt, Rameses I died in 1295 BC in Memphis.

SETI I

King Seti I was now in charge of the mummification and burial of his father. Unfortunately, the craftsmen in the Valley of the Kings had not had enough time to complete his tomb. Therefore, in the seventy days traditionally set aside for the embalming process, a much smaller version of the tomb for Rameses I was quickly finished.

Seti I and his son Rameses, who was now about eight or nine, sailed south from Memphis to Luxor accompanying the mummified body of

Rameses I. People lined the banks of the river to watch both the passing of the old king and to catch a glimpse of their new ruler. On arrival at the west bank at Luxor, the king's body was taken off the royal barge, to the sounds of ritual prayers sung by priests and loud wailing from women who were specially paid as professional mourners. A proces-

A portrait of Seti I, the father of Rameses II, from Seti's wooden sarcophagus.

sion then led from the banks of the river Nile to the memorial temple of Rameses I, and then secretly on to the tomb of the king hidden in the Valley of the Kings. Here special rituals were performed by Seti and accompanying priests in front of the body of his father before the mummified figure was lowered into his coffin and the tomb was sealed.

After performing these rituals, Seti took the opportunity to pick out the site in the Valley of the Kings for his own tomb, and he ordered craftsmen to begin carving it out of the hillside. He also began the construction of his own memorial temple on the west bank. He and the child Rameses also visited the great temple to Amen at Karnak to check on the building work of the hypostyle hall. Seti now ordered that his name be carved everywhere, and that the hall should be called "Effective is Seti I in the domain of Amen." He also decided that the outsides of the walls, which more people would see, should be covered with scenes of Seti I beating all his enemies in battle.

On the way back to Memphis, Seti and young Rameses stopped off at Abydos, which was the center of the cult of Osiris, who was the most important god of the afterlife. Here Seti commissioned the construction of an unusual temple that would contain seven separate cult sanctuaries for the worship of all the important gods of Egypt. This building would also have a list of most of the previous kings of Egypt carved on its walls, and it is now famous for being the site of some of the most beautiful carvings from ancient Egypt. At the same time, Seti ordered the building of a smaller temple for his father Rameses I and a slightly larger one for his son Rameses. Back in the capital, Seti ordered improvements at the great temple to the god Ptah at Memphis and the temple of the sun god Ra at Heliopolis. Seti's hometown was not forgotten, and in the eastern Delta he ordered the construction of a fine summer palace decorated with blue and white tiles.

Now that Seti I was in charge, he was able to pursue his ambition of restoring Egypt's control of Canaan and Syria by beating all the local princes and chieftains who had taken the opportunity to rebel against Egypt toward the end of the Eighteenth Dynasty. Seti proclaimed that the tribal chiefs "have lapsed into confusion and quarreling; each slays his fellow. They ignore the laws of the Palace."

Seti conducted a series of campaigns that are known as the Northern Wars. In year one of his reign (Egyptian years started over again at the beginning of each new king's reign), the Egyptian army marched from the northeast Delta across the Sinai desert as far as Gaza in the region of Canaan (in modern Israel). Here they fought an enormous battle with the local tribe who were called the Shasu. The royal scribes wrote, "His Majesty seized upon them like a terrifying lion, turning them into corpses throughout their valleys, wallowing in their blood as if they had never existed." Seti then marched on as far as Beth Shan on the Jordan

A limestone *stela*, or stone tablet, showing Rameses as a child.

River, where he set up a *stela* (stone tablet) to commemorate another victory. It reads "His Majesty sent out the First Division of Amen, 'Rich in Bows,' against the town of Hammath; the First Division of Ra, 'Abounding in Valor,' against the town of Beth Shan; and the First Division of Seth, 'Strong of Bows,' against the town of Yenoam. And so, when the span of a day had elapsed, they were all fallen to the might of his Majesty."

In the next two years, Seti and his army returned again to Canaan and Syria and tried to finish the job of making peace and strengthening Egypt's hold on the region. His armies also secured for Egypt the coastal ports of Tyre, Sidon, Byblos, and Simyra.

The other great superpower at this time was the Hittite empire, which was based in Hatti (modern Turkey) in the north. This power also controlled territory spreading southward toward the Egyptian-controlled areas. King Seti and the Hittite king Muwatallis fought briefly in year four (1291 BC). This was the beginning of a long series of conflicts between them.

PRINCE RAMESES

But what of Rameses? Although by age ten he had been made Crown Prince and Commander in Chief of the Army, he was actually left safely at home in Memphis during these campaigns.

He lived for most of the year with his mother, Tuya, and his sisters, Tiya and Hetmire, in the royal palace in the capital city of Memphis. The family went for holidays to their palace at Ghurob in the Faiyum. This location had been a favorite of royal families since the Middle Kingdom, and was famous for its beautiful gardens and lakes.

Since the Eighteenth Dynasty, there had been a special palace here for the royal women, some of whom lived there all year round. Others, such as Queen Tuya, her daughters, and Rameses' wives, went for visits. The royal ladies ran a very lively and bustling palace compound, effectively a small town that was famous for making very fine linen used to make the royal family's clothes.

Rameses enjoyed hunting fish and birds in the lake and the marshes. In the hot summer months the family also visited their palace at Avaris in the northeast Delta near the Mediterranean coast.

Rameses went to school with other boys in the palace compound at Memphis to learn reading, writing, and mathematics. One of his teachers there was a man called Tia, who later married Rameses' sister Tiya. The couple was eventually buried in a joint tomb that has recently been discovered at Saqqara.

Sports were also an important part of a boy's education. Rameses learned how to use a bow and arrow, and how to shoot targets while riding on a chariot. He also developed his strength by riding horses and wrestling with other boys.

Military training usually took place in special army camps, where soldiers learned how to drill and to use different weapons. As crown prince, Rameses had his own special training, but often visited these camps as part of his duties as commander-in-chief.

In year four of Seti's reign, when Rameses was thirteen, the opportunity arose for him to accompany the Egyptian army for the first time. While Seti was dealing with the Hittites in the north, Libyan raiding parties from the country to the west were causing trouble in the western Delta of Egypt. Seti hurried back to Egypt and, taking Rameses with him, conducted a brief but successful campaign to repel the Libyans. He was proclaimed he "who overthrows those who rebel against him, who smites the tribes people and tramples down the Bedouin and the distant foreign lands of Libya, making great slaughter amongst them."

Rameses almost certainly watched the battle only from a distance, as his father would not have wanted to put him in danger. But the prince is shown for the first time standing next to his father in the battle scenes carved on the walls of the temples in Karnak.

The next year Seti went back to Syria to continue his battle against King Muwatallis, and this time he took Rameses with him. The armies fought over an important city in northern Syria called Kadesh. Seti briefly won control of the city and erected a victory *stela*, most of which is now lost. However, Muwatallis fought back, and the two kings finally agreed to a truce where Egypt would keep all the coastal ports that Seti had previously won, but the Hittites would keep Kadesh. These battles, and the victory at Kadesh that soon turned to defeat, had a profound effect on young Prince Rameses. He never forgot that Kadesh had once been Egyptian and he was determined that one day he would win it back.

RAMESES AS REGENT

Prince Rameses also accompanied his father in the course of performing royal duties inside Egypt. Together they went on regular inspections of the new buildings being built in the important cities at Luxor, Abydos, and Memphis. Rameses also learned how to run the administration of the government and the civil service.

During year seven, 1289 BC, when Rameses was sixteen, Seti decided to announce to the whole country that Prince Rameses was definitely the heir to the throne and would one day be the next pharaoh. This was a sensible step. The Rameses family was still quite new to the throne, and Seti wanted to ensure that there would be no doubt in the minds of the army and the government that Rameses was an important person whom they should obey.

A painting of a farmer and his wife plowing a garden in the afterlife.

Consequently, an important ceremony was arranged where Rameses was crowned prince regent. The event is described by Rameses himself in an inscription on the wall of his father's temple at Abydos:

It was Menmaatre [Seti] who brought me up. The Lord of All himself magnified me, while I was still a child, until I became ruler. He assigned me the land while I was yet in the egg. The officials paid homage to me when I was installed as Senior Prince . . . When my father appeared before the populace, I being just a youth in his embrace, he spoke thus concerning me, "Crown him as king that I may see his beauty while I yet live!" He had the Chamberlains summoned to set the crowns upon my brow . . . so he said of me, while he was yet on this earth, "He shall govern this land, he shall care for its boundaries, he shall give commands to the people." He spoke of me, his eyes filled with tears, so great was the love for me within him. He furnished me with a household from the Royal Harem, comparable with the beauties of the Palace. He selected for me wives throughout the land.

The royal titles of the pharaoh were made up of five "great names," which he received on the day of his coronation. The particular identity and interests of the king were often reflected in the names selected. The last two names of the king, known as the prenomen and nomen, were enclosed in oval or oblong decorative frames called cartouches.

The prenomen was the pharaoh's formal name and was used for things like official statements and foreign dealings. The nomen was the pharaoh's personal name and the one that was used by his family and friends. Rameses now had to choose what his five throne names would be.

The first three names he chose were "The Horus, Mighty Bull, Beloved of Maat," "He of Two Ladies, Conqueror of Foreign Lands," and "Horus of Gold, Rich in Years, Great in Victories." All of these show the emphasis that Rameses placed on his own and Egypt's military strength and power. Seti's last names were Menmaatre, "Enduring is the Maat of Ra," and Seti-Meryptah, "Seti Beloved of Ptah." Rameses modeled his names on those of his father and called himself Usermaatre, "Strong is the Maat of Ra," and Rameses-Meryamen, "Rameses, Beloved of Ra."

Female musicians, from a painting in the tomb of Rekhmire, a governor of Thebes.

Rameses' home life now changed. His father had given him his own household with his own wives and concubines. This meant that he now moved from the main palace where his parents lived into another palace on the same grounds. Here, at the age of sixteen, he lived with his own servants, some of whom were childhood friends who had grown up with him in the palace compound. One of his best friends, Ameneminet, was now appointed his personal companion. Another friend and servant was Menna, who was Rameses' shieldbearer, a sort of bodyguard. When Rameses rode in a chariot, Menna would go with him to protect him.

The wives provided for him were well-brought up Egyptian girls from high-ranking families selected by Seti and his advisors as suitable partners for the future king. There were probably also some foreign girls who were the daughters of princes and chiefs from Canaan and Syria who wanted to please Seti. Unlike previous pharaohs, the first Rameses kings did not marry their own sisters. This was because Rameses I and Seti I did not actually come from a royal family, and to them the idea would have seemed rather peculiar. Rameses II, however, was later to marry at least four of his own daughters.

Rameses' two main wives were Nefertari and Iset Nofret. We do not know very much about either of these women, except that they were both about the same age as Rameses and probably both from Egyptian families.

In a very short time, Nefertari had a son called Amenhirwonmef, and then Iset Nofret had a son called Rameses. Nefertari then had another son called Prehirwonmef and a daughter called Bint-Anath, while Iset Nofret had another son called Khaemwaset.

Other lesser wives also bore Rameses children, and eventually he had nearly forty children!

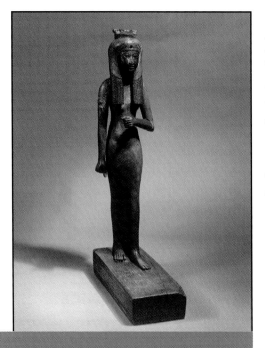

A small wooden statue of Queen Nefertari, the wife of Rameses II.

Even though Rameses had now been declared joint king with his father, everyone knew that Seti was still the king and that Rameses was his deputy, who did what his father told him to do. For the next few years Seti and Rameses focused on domestic affairs. Seti spent most of his time running the government of the country from Memphis. He and his wife Tuya went for holidays to his summer palace at Avaris in the northeast Delta. In the winter they went to Luxor, where they lived in palaces, now lost, near the main temple at Karnak and also on the west bank at his memorial temple at Gurna.

Rameses spent his time traveling up and down the country keeping an eye on all the building projects that had been commissioned by his father. As part of his training, he was sometimes trusted to lead royal missions on his own. In year nine, for example, when Rameses was eighteen years old, he was put in charge of an expedition to the granite quarries at Aswan, in the southern part of the country. This expedition was sent to mine a special kind of black granite that was used to make statues and obelisks to decorate the temples and palaces being built by Seti. The royal scribes wrote:

> His Majesty commissioned a multitude of works, to make very great obelisks and great and marvelous statues in the name of His Majesty. He constructed great barges for transporting them, with ships' crews to match them, ferrying them from their quarry, with high officials and transport men hastening the work along. And his senior son [Rameses] was before them, doing good service for His Majesty.

Rameses was also now thought experienced enough to lead the army on his own. In year thirteen, 1283 BC, when Rameses was twenty-two, there was some unrest among the local population in northern Nubia. Rameses, along with his two sons, Amenhirwonmef (aged five) and Khaemwaset (aged four), went to Nubia and quickly subdued the unhappy Nubians.

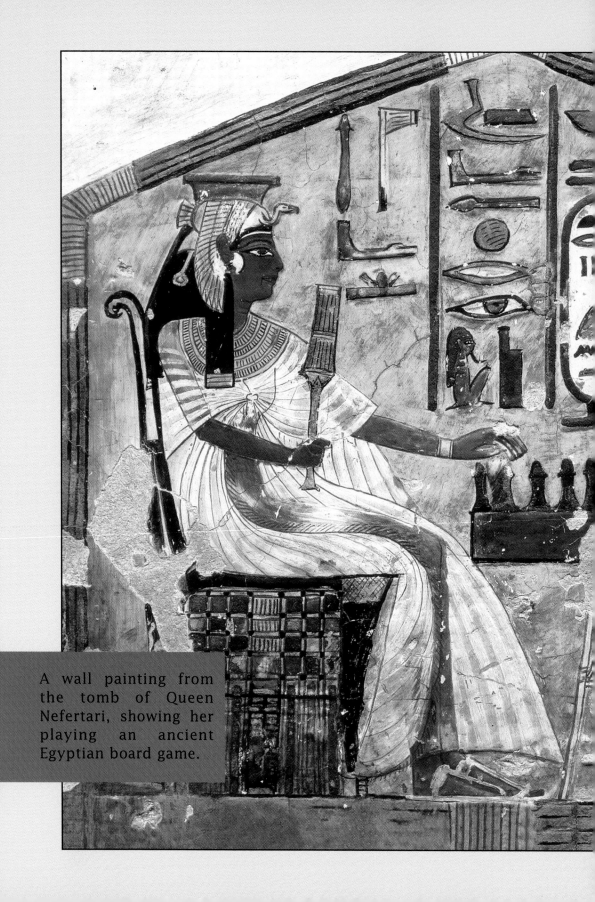

A wall painting from the tomb of Queen Nefertari, showing her playing an ancient Egyptian board game.

Scenes that Rameses later had carved on the walls of a small temple at Beit el Wali near the site of the battle show Rameses and his sons, each in their own chariot with a shieldbearer, charging against the enemy, who are shown running away. A Nubian women cries, "We have never known such raging of a ruler, he is like Seth in the sky!"

The next few years passed comparatively quietly. All the great building works progressed, and a few matters of unrest, including incidents of piracy in the Mediterranean, were quickly dealt with. Rameses continued to learn from his father about all the duties associated with being ruler of Egypt. In the summer of year sixteen, 1279 BC, when Rameses was twenty-five years old, King Seti suddenly died while he and his wife Tuya were on holiday at his summer palace at Avaris.

A large statue of Rameses II with Queen Nefertari as a small figure at his feet, from the temple of Karnak at Luxor.

KING RAMESES

Rameses was now king. This was the moment for which he had been trained almost his whole life. He was a tall, good-looking man, with a prominent nose, high cheekbones, almond-shaped eyes, a fleshy mouth, and a small, square chin. He also had large ears and red hair, which was unusual. He was fit and healthy, and skilled in all the arts of running the government. He controlled a great country that stretched from the provinces of Nubia in the south to Canaan and Syria in the north.

However, Rameses' first task was to oversee the burial of his father, King Seti. Messengers were sent from Avaris to Thebes to warn the craftsmen who were finishing the king's tomb and all the pieces of equipment that were traditionally buried with the king. Meanwhile the embalmers at Avaris were busy preparing the king's body. Rameses and his mother, Tuya, stayed in the Delta, while news of the new king was sent around the country. While still at Avaris, Rameses also announced that this was to be the site of a new city that he was going to build as the new capital of Egypt. It would be called Piramesse Anakhtu, which meant "Home of Rameses the Victorious." As when he chose his five throne names, this was another indication that Rameses wanted, above all else, to be thought of as a successful warrior.

In August 1279 BC, Rameses set off from Avaris with the body of his father, accompanied by his mother, his sisters, his major wives, and some of his children. They traveled in a group of boats or barges, which were the most common form of transport in a country where most movement happened on the river rather than by road. Boats were either sailed or powered by oarsmen or towed forward with ropes from the bank. Their first stop was at Heliopolis, which was the cult center of the sun god Ra. Along with Amen, Ra was the most important god during the New Kingdom. After saying prayers and making offerings to the god, the royal family then moved on to the capital at Memphis. The government was based

Masons making bricks.

there, and the impor-tant officials were given the chance to say good-bye to the old king and to recognize Rameses as their new ruler.

All the ships containing Rameses' family as well as the priests and important officials set sail for Thebes. After Seti's body was unloaded, it was carried to his memorial temple at Gurna on the river plain on the west bank at Thebes. Here, there was a big religious service that everyone attended. After this, a smaller group of just the most important priests and members of the family followed the coffin into the desert to the Valley of the Kings. They were probably followed by a long procession of priests and others carrying all the things that would go into the tomb with the dead king. These burial items included four canopic jars containing different parts of the king's body that had been removed during mummification. Each canopic jar had a lid representing one of the four sons of Horus, who were guardians of the entrails. Imset had a human head and guarded the liver, Hapy had a baboon head and guarded the lungs, Qebhsenuef had a falcon head and guarded the intestines, and Duamutef had a jackal head and guarded the stomach.

The technique of mummification developed throughout Egyptian history was, by the time of the New Kingdom, a very efficient way of preserving the body. Good samples of preserved remains from this period still exist. The body of Seti I has been badly damaged, but his head is remarkably well preserved, and his mummy can be seen today in the Cairo Museum. Seti's tomb contained a huge granite sarcophagus, or outer box, that his coffin was lowered into. He also had a very beautiful inner sarcophagus made of alabaster and covered with carved scenes from the Book of Gates, colored with blue pigment. All the rooms and passages of the tomb were beautifully decorated with religious texts written in hieroglyphics and pictures of the king with various gods. Many objects were also put into the tomb in case the king needed them in his afterlife. These included furniture, clothes, food, jewelry, weapons, and books, as well as many objects of religious importance. Unfortunately his tomb was repeatedly robbed quite soon after he was buried, so we can only guess at the original splendor.

After all the objects had been placed in the tomb, Rameses and the high priests conducted the final religious ceremonies with the body and lowered Seti's coffin into place. The tomb was then closed and the door sealed.

After the funeral, Rameses and his family stayed on in Luxor. The most important religious event in Luxor was called the Festival of Opet, which took place once a year. The main event of this festival was the carrying of the statues of the gods in procession from Karnak Temple to Luxor Temple. These statues traveled in "barks" that were shaped like little Nile River boats. The prow and stern of each boat showed the head of the particular god, while the statue itself was hidden in a shrine in the middle of the vessel. Common people weren't

This painting from the tomb of Nakht, the keeper of the king's vineyards and granaries, depicts woodcutters at work.

allowed to actually see the gods, as this was reserved for the king and the priests. Pictures in temples show us that these barks were often carried by rows of priests. The purpose of this festival was to celebrate the symbolic mating of the god Amen

with the mother of the king, reinforcing the idea that the king was son of the gods.

This was the first time that Rameses was the focus of the festival. He traveled with the sacred barks from Karnak Temple to Luxor Temple with a huge procession of priests. The river edges were lined with thousands of people—soldiers, musicians, and dancers—who followed the barges from the banks. Rameses was taken by a group of priests to the dark inner sanctuary of the temple where the image of the god was kept. There, in flickering candlelight and accompanied by prayers and burning incense, the king was symbolically joined to the new *ka*, or life force, created by the god. The climax of the festival was when Rameses reemerged to cheering crowds as if transformed into a god himself.

A gold statuette of Rameses II

This festival was a very important event for Rameses, as it ensured that the mystic role of kingship continued even when the royal family didn't. Ay, Horemheb, Rameses I, and Seti I had all undertaken the same ritual, and the Opet festival had managed to merge all the kings into one royal line. Although Rameses had inherited the throne from his father and did not have to worry about being of royal blood, it was still very reassuring to know that the god Amen had also recognized him as the true ruler.

The Opet festival was also a time when important government matters were often discussed. Priests were chosen for promotion to fill the jobs of older priests who had died. Political promotions also took place. Rameses' friend Amrneminet was promoted to royal charioteer and superintendent of horses.

Royal inspections were also conducted. Rameses checked on the progress of his tomb in the Valley of the Kings and finished off Seti's memorial temple on the west bank.

He also began planning his own memorial temple, which today is known as the Ramesseum. This was the main building from which the funerary cult of Rameses would operate after his death. In other words, it would be a large temple dedicated to the king and the location of offerings made by a large group of priests for his *ka*, or spirit, after he had died. His memorial temple would have a floor plan similar to other New Kingdom temples, but in this case there would also be a statue of Rameses in the inner sanctuary. The temple would actually form one part of a small town, all enclosed by a high mud brick wall. Other buildings included a palace for Rameses to stay in when he visited, a school for training religious and government scribes, a library, and many large granaries and warehouses where goods were stored.

On the east bank, the hypostyle hall at Karnak was still under construction, and Rameses changed the name once again to "Effective is Rameses II in Amen's Domain." He also decided to enlarge the neighboring Luxor

A decorated wooden
cosmetic case recovered
from Memphis

Temple by adding a new pylon gateway and a large open courtyard with columns around the edges. Rameses decreed that there would be a large statue of himself in between each column, as well as four large seated statues flanking the doorways. After ensuring that all these expensive and elaborate buildings were underway, in October 1297 BC, Rameses and his family set sail northward back to the capital at Memphis.

War with Syria

The next few years passed swiftly, with Rameses attending to the actual business of ruling the country. At some point, in year two of his reign (1278 BC), he decided to alter his prenomen or throne name, which now became Usermaatre Setepenre, "Strong in Right is Ra, Chosen by Ra, Rameses Meryamen." He kept a close watch on the building projects in Memphis, Abydos, and Luxor. The king's dynamic activity is mirrored in the rather boastful inscriptions carved on the walls of his temples. In the Karnak Temple one inscription reads "It was his majesty who gave the regulations and led the work on his monuments. All his plans came to pass immediately."

In theory, Rameses was in charge of every aspect of the government. One of his main duties was to ensure the prosperity of the country. It should be remembered that construction on such a massive scale was very expensive. The king's treasury had to support all the workmen involved in the building of the temples. Fortunately, the Egyptians had plenty of gold. Egypt was famous in the ancient world as a source of the precious metal, and about 200 years before, the king of Mitanni had written to King Amenhotep III that "In my brother's country [Egypt], gold is as plentiful as dirt."

The Egyptians obtained gold from the deserts to the east of the Nile Valley and also from Nubian deserts in the south. Mining and quarrying expeditions were carried out under military control, and the king was supposedly the only person who was allowed to order the work. Many of the laborers were convicts and being sent to the gold mines was often as bad as a death sentence, as working conditions were very difficult and dangerous.

Gold was usually extracted from veins running through the mineral quartz. Fires were lit inside the mines, which heated and cracked the face of the rock. Men then broke pieces off with hammers and picks. Lumps of rock were carried outside the mine, where they were first crushed by large stone mortars and then ground into a fine powder. This powder was washed in water in flat pans so that the fragments of gold, which are heavier than the particles of rock, sank to the bottom of the pan. These fragments were then melted into small ingots.

Reports had reached Rameses that there was a rich source of gold at a particular spot in Nubia, but that it was almost impossible to work there. The reports said that "there is much gold in the land of Akuyati, but the road is extremely difficult because of the water problem. Of the gold prospectors who went there, only half of them ever arrived there, for they died of thirst on the way along with the donkeys that went before them. There could not be found for them their needs for drinking, either going or coming back."

Rameses summoned all his advisors to discuss the issue, stating proudly that "I shall take the matter in hand." He sent a detailed list of instructions to the viceroy of Nubia for an ambitious well-building program, defying all past experience with the region, saying, "Water has never been struck in this territory since the time of the God, as you say. But I shall open up a well there yielding water daily." The program was obviously successful, because a couple of months later the viceroy sent another letter that said, "Everything has happened just as your majesty said with his own mouth. Water appeared in the well at twelve cubits [eighteen feet] . . . Never has anything like it happened before. The chief of Akuyati rejoiced immensely. Those who were far off marveled and came to see the well created by the Ruler." The well was duly named "The Well of Rameses II, Valiant in Deeds."

WAR

In year four (1275 BC) of his reign, Rameses felt strong enough to turn to a problem that had rankled him since he was a boy. He had vivid memories of his father Seti's campaigns in Syria against Muwatallis, the emperor of the Hittites. In particular, he remembered the unsatisfactory stalemate reached at the city of Kadesh. Kadesh and the region of Amurru had been Egyptian territory since the reign of Tuthmose III, 200 years before. These areas were lost during the reign of Akhenaten about a hundred years before. Rameses now decided to reconquer this region of modern-day Syria and perhaps even expand Egypt's empire into new territories to the north. He and his armies set off first for the coastal cities of Tyre and

Byblos, which were already under Egyptian control, and from there he quickly overwhelmed the region of Amurru farther up the coast, though he did not reach the city of Kadesh, which was farther inland.

The ruler of Amurru, called Prince Benteshina, was in theory a subject of the Hittite emperor, but he had no choice but to submit to Rameses and to declare that Amurru would now come under Egyptian control and pay taxes to Egypt instead. Rameses was not just fuelled by romantic ideas of restoring the Egyptian empire. He was also motivated by the practical consideration of getting more money for the Egyptian treasury as well. However, Benteshina was afraid that Muwatallis would be furious with him, so he wrote a secret letter to the Hittite emperor saying that he had switched allegiance to Egypt, but that he had been forced to do so and had no choice in the matter. Rameses and his armies set off back to Egypt to celebrate these victories, and also to plan the next campaign against Kadesh and other cities farther inland.

Muwatallis was furious. He had received the letter from Benteshina and quickly realized that the young pharaoh Rameses was serious in his pursuit of northern territory. Muwatallis decided that Rameses needed to be taught a lesson. He vowed to the gods of Hatti that he would recover Amurru, stop the Egyptians from taking Kadesh, and chase Rameses all the way back to Egypt.

PREPARING FOR BATTLE

During the spring of 1274 BC, Muwatallis assembled a massive army. Egyptian records suggest that the Hittites managed to gather together 2,500 chariots and 37,000 men. The royal scribes wrote:

> Now the vile foe from Hatti had come and brought together all the foreign lands as far as the end of the sea. The entire land of Hatti had come, that of Nahrin also, that of Arzawa and Dardany, that of Keshkesh, those of Masa, those of Pidasa, that of Irun, that of Karkisha, that of Luka, Kizzuwadna, Carcamesh, Ugarit, Kedy, the entire land of Nuges, Mushanet, and Kadesh. He had not spared a country from being brought, of all those distant lands, and their chiefs were there with him, each one with his infantry and chariots, a great number without equal. They covered the mountains and

valleys and were like locusts in their multi-tude. He had left no silver in his land. He had stripped it of all its possessions and had given them to all the foreign countries in order to bring them with him to fight.

Rameses prepared his army at Piramesse in the eastern Delta. Archaeological evidence indi-cates that massive metal smelting works were established at the barracks in the city. From these, thousands of axes, arrowheads, spear-heads, knives, and swords were hurriedly pro-duced. We also know that chariots were manufactured here, and that hundreds, if not thousands, of horses were stabled and trained as well.

Along with the weapons that had been in use since the Old Kingdom, which included spears, axes, and bows and arrows, there were a number of technical innovations in the New Kingdom.

The horse-drawn chariot, first introduced by the Hyksos rulers of the Second Intermediate Period, was now the chosen conveyance of rich, young Egyptians. The king was also often shown on temple walls fighting from a chariot. Body armor, made from small bronze plates sewn onto linen or leather jackets was also now in use, and a leather sample was found in the tomb of Tutankhamen. Bows were now made from goat horn and bone glued to wood, and these were more powerful and could shoot arrows much farther—more than 300 yards—than bows made from wood alone. A special dagger, a sword with a curved blade, called a *khepesh* was invented at this time.

It was decided that Rameses and the bulk of the army would march overland from the eastern Delta toward Kadesh, while a supporting force would sail up the coast and march inland to meet up with the pharaoh. Rameses set off leading an army of 20,000 men and chariots. The army was divided into four divisions of 5,000 soldiers each. These divisions were named Amen (probably made up of men from the Theban region), Ra (from Heliopolis), Ptah (from Memphis), and Seth (from the eastern Delta). Rameses was also accompanied by one of the two viziers, some of his sons, his household staff, and his personal bodyguard. The troops and horses and chariots were accompanied by pack animals and ox-drawn carts carrying food, water, weapons, tents, and other necessary provisions. Ramses' scribes recorded:

> His majesty journeyed northward, his infantry and chariots with him. He began

the march well, in year five, the second month of summer, on day nine. His majesty passed the fortress of Sile [on the Egyptian side of the Sinai desert], being mighty like the god Montu when he appears, all foreign lands trembling before him, their chiefs bringing their gifts, and all rebels coming bowed down through fear of his majesty's might.

After a month's travel, the army reached Kumidi. Then Rameses and his household troops and personal bodyguard and the division of Amen set off northward toward the Orontes River, which they had to cross in order to reach the city of Kadesh. The other three divisions followed behind, and the army stretched back for many miles.

As they marched through the woods of Labwi, two Bedouin tribesmen were found hiding in the trees. They said that they were deserters from the Hittite army, and had come to fight for Rameses. "We will be servants of Pharaoh and will abandon the chief of Hatti." They also told the king that the massive Hittite army was 120 miles farther north. "The foe from Hatti is in the land of Aleppo to the north of Tunip. He was too fearful of Pharaoh to come southward when he heard that the pharaoh had come northward." Rameses and his advisers were pleased by this news, because it indicated that they would be able to conquer Kadesh without much opposition. They and the Amen division crossed the river, rode north toward the city, and began to set up camp on the plain to the west.

However, as Rameses set up camp with the Amen division, and as the Ra division marched up the plain toward the camp, and as the Ptah and Seth divisions prepared to ford the river to the south, disaster struck. The army had been lulled into a false sense of security by the information from the captured Bedouins that the Hittite army was still many days' travel away. Scouts sent out from Rameses' camp now captured two Hittite spies near the city of Kadesh, and they were brought before the pharaoh, though probably tortured first. "His majesty said to them 'What are you?' They replied 'We belong to the ruler of Hatti. He sent us to see where your Majesty was.' His majesty said to them 'Where is he, the Foe from Hatti? I have heard that he is in the land of Aleppo north of Tunip.' They replied, 'Behold, the Ruler of Hatti has already come, together with the many foreign lands that he brought as

This wall carving depicts the pharaoh's officers beating Hittite spies to make them confess at the Battle of Kadesh.

allies . . . They are equipped with their infantry and their chariots and their weapons of war. They are more numerous than the grains of sand on the beach. See, they are poised armed and ready to fight behind Kadesh!'"

This was a disaster! The Hittite army was not 120 miles away, but could attack at any moment. Rameses was furious at the uselessness of his intelligence services and summoned his chief officers to tell them the appalling news. "See what state my provincial governors and high officers are in, that they go round saying daily 'Oh, the Hittite ruler is in Aleppo, away north of Tunip! But now, this very hour, have I heard from these two Hittite spies, that the Hittite ruler has already come with his allies, his innumerable troops. Even now they are poised hidden behind Kadesh, and the generals and officers in charge of my territories were unable to tell us that they had come!"

FIGHTING COMMENCES

In the camp of the Amen division countermeasures were taken as quickly as possible. The vizier was sent galloping off to the Ptah and Seth divisions to tell them to hurry across the river, while the royal family, who had accompanied the king to the site of the battle, fled westward out of danger under the leadership of Prince Prehirwonmef.

All of these hasty preparations were observed by the Hittite army under the command of Muwatallis. His army was concealed on the east bank of the river opposite the city. They had seen the Egyptian king and the Amen division arrive at the site. They could also see the Ra division straggling across the plain. The sight of the vizier galloping south was probably just the sign they were waiting for. The time was right to attack.

Suddenly a massive force of chariots, led by several Hittite princes, dashed westward across the river south of the city and headed toward the Egyptian army, still partly strung out along its line of march. The Ra division was taken by complete surprise. The soldiers forgot all their military training in the panic, and instead of fighting back they scattered and fled north, leading the enemy right into the Egyptian camp.

Seeing the distraught soldiers and the huge dust cloud of enemy chariots heading toward them, many of the Amen division also lost their heads and rushed around in confusion. The

Hittite chariots swept around the camp and burst through the defensive line of shields along the western side of the camp. All seemed lost. Rameses' army was being wiped out all around him, and it seemed more than likely that he himself would be captured or killed by the enemy.

A wall carving showing Rameses in his chariot drawing a bow.

Rameses threw on his armor and leapt onto his chariot. In vain he tried to rally his panicked troops, but he was ready to fight to the death. He later told his version of the events that followed:

> When Menna my shieldbearer saw that a large number of chariots surrounded me, he became weak and faint-hearted, great fear invading his body. He cried out to his majesty "My good lord, mighty prince, we stand alone in the midst of

battle, abandoned by soldiers and chariots, why do you stay to save them? Let us
get clear, save us Usermaatre Setepenre!"
His majesty said to his shieldbearer
"Stand firm, steady yourself, my shieldbearer! I shall go for them like the
pounce of a falcon, killing, slaughtering,
and felling them to the ground." His
majesty then rushed forward, at a gallop
he charged into the midst of the foe. I
was after them like Baal [the Syrian war
god] in his moment of power, I slew them
without pause.

Rameses managed to stay alive and hold
off the Hittite attack while his troops were
panicking. It is not clear how long he would
have managed on his own, but in the next
moment help arrived. The division of soldiers
who had sailed to the Syrian coast and
marched eastward inland to join up with the
royal army suddenly appeared on the scene.
The division immediately began to attack the
Hittite charioteers.

The Hittites now found themselves caught
between a furious Rameses and a brand-new
army arriving from the west. The extra troops
came as a complete surprise to the Hittites,

whose spies were obviously not much better than the Egyptian ones.

Together, Rameses and the new division managed to push the Hittites back away from the camp. The Hittites, now wondering if any more Egyptian divisions were about to appear, suddenly turned and fled back toward the river and the main Hittite camp to the east.

Muwatallis had stayed behind at the Hittite camp, and as he heard the sounds of battle in the distance he probably imagined that the Egyptians were being soundly beaten. He must have been very shocked to see the Hittite chariots being chased into the river by Egyptian troops with the Pharaoh leading them. Before Muwatallis's horrified gaze, the Hittite army struggled into the water, with princes and soldiers alike swimming for their lives. A scene on the walls of the Ramesseum even shows that Rebeyer, the prince of Aleppo, swallowed so much river water on the way across that his retainers had to hold him upside down by the ankles to empty the water out.

As the Hittites struggled back to their camp, the Ptah division finally arrived, led by the vizier, and the stragglers and disorganized elements from the Amen and Ra divisions

A *stela* carving showing Rameses holding Nubian, Libyan, and Syrian prisoners by the hair.

slipped back into the Egyptian camp. The Seth division finally arrived later that night.

THE AFTERMATH

Both rulers spent the evening assessing the damage to their armies. The Amen and Ra divisions had suffered many casualties, but the Ptah and Seth divisions were still intact, as was the bulk of the support force. The two Hittite infantry divisions, more than 30,000 troops altogether, were unharmed, but the chariot division had suffered many losses. Sadly for Muwatallis, many of his army leaders had been killed in battle or drowned, and the losses included two of the emperor's brothers, two of his shieldbearers, his secretary, and the chief of his bodyguard.

The two largest armies ever seen now faced each other across the Orontes River. Large-scale open battle between rival armies was not the normal type of warfare during this period. The Egyptians were used to overpowering smaller states one at a time, while the Hittites preferred to ambush their enemies. Nevertheless, early the next morning Rameses attacked the Hittite camp in force. Without chariots the Hittites could not push the Egyptians back, but

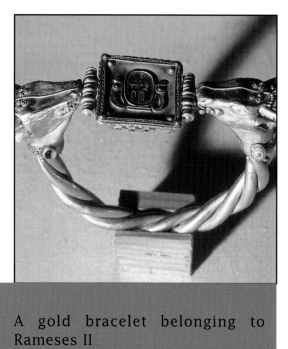

A gold bracelet belonging to Rameses II

Muwatallis's army was much larger than Rameses' and they stood their ground. No one could win this battle, and the Egyptian army finally disengaged.

As he had done fifteen years before with Seti I, Muwatallis now sent a letter containing peace proposals to the Egyptian camp. The letter ended, "Peace is better than fighting. Give us breath!" Rameses summoned another meeting of his chief officers and read them the letter. A truce was finally agreed upon, and Rameses and his armies returned to Egypt to celebrate the "victory."

Rameses was so proud of this campaign that he had versions of the story carved on the walls of many temples in Egypt, including the temples at Karnak, Luxor, the Ramesseum, Abydos, and Abu Simbel. It is worth remembering, however, that he didn't actually achieve what he had set out to. Kadesh was not conquered or captured, and Amurru fell back under Hittite control. Poor Prince Benteshina was deposed from the throne and sent into exile in Hatti, where he ended up as the servant to the emperor's brother Hattusil. As for Muwatallis, he had stopped the Egyptians from expanding northward, but he had also lost many close friends. Furthermore, Adadnirari I, the king of Assyria, had taken the opportunity to steal a piece of the Hittite empire called Hanigalbat while the Hittites were occupied with the Egyptians.

During 1273 BC Rameses concentrated his efforts on rebuilding his army at home. However, many of the Egyptian subjects in Caanan and Syria took this as a sign of weakness and began to disobey Egyptian orders. They stopped paying taxes.

In the spring of 1272 BC Rameses once more turned his attentions to the north. He marched to Gaza and swiftly beat off marauding bands of Bedouin tribesmen who had been causing unrest. His eldest son, Prince Amenhirwonmef, who had now changed his name to Amenhirkhopshef, led another army north, and between them they reasserted Egyptian power in Canaan. The next year (1271 BC) Rameses led the army north again. He advanced as far as Tunip, but he avoided Amurru and the city of Kadesh. He left a statue of himself in the main temple at the city of Dapur, and then returned to Egypt in triumph.

Why had the Hittites not responded to this second provocative invasion? The reason was that after many years on the Hittite throne, Muwatallis had died. He was succeeded by his unpopular son, Uri-Teshub, who ruled as Mursill III, and who was busy at home in a political struggle with his powerful uncle, Hattusil. Nevertheless Tunip returned to Hittite rule as soon as Rameses had left, and in year ten (1269 BC) Rameses returned to Dapur once more. These yearly campaigns continued until the situation was finally resolved in year twenty-one.

Margins of Empire

Rameses now turned his attention to Nubia in the south. He had ordered the construction of two temples to be carved into a hillside on the west bank of the Nile a few miles south of Aksha. One was to have four colossal statues of the king carved out of the rockface, and the other was dedicated to the goddess Hathor and the king's wife Nefertari. The front of this temple was to be decorated with alternating statues of the king and queen. Rameses dispatched an old friend, Ashahebsed, to take over affairs in Nubia and oversee the work on the temples.

Between the years ten and eighteen there are few documents that tell us what the king was doing. Although the temples built by Rameses II are covered with scenes of wars with enemies both north and south, it is not always easy to tell exactly what is happening. It is clear

The entrance to the temple of Rameses II at Luxor, Egypt

that at some time around the year twenty some of the Nubians rebelled and tried to get rid of their Egyptian rulers. Rameses sent an army led by his sons Setemwia and Merenptah to help the viceroy of Nubia. Egypt quickly defeated the rebels, and 7,000 captives were taken back to Egypt. To celebrate the victory, a new city was built at Amara called "Rameses the Town." Rameses ordered the construction of a number of temples in Nubia at Beit el-Wali, Gerf Hussein, Wadi el-Sebua, and Ed-Derr.

In Egypt, Rameses was viewed by his people as a human king who was also a kind of god as the son of Osiris and the representative of Horus on Earth. In Nubia, however, Rameses was portrayed as a true god. The Nubians were a conquered people firmly under the control of the Egyptian state, and it was to be expected in this situation that the dominant power would use frightening and overwhelming images to reinforce fear of the victor's power.

Massive statues of the king as god were carved to strike fear and obedience into the local population, with any religious significance a secondary consideration. It is also clear, because of the way Rameses was increasingly portrayed as a god in temples built later and later in his reign, that the notion of his own divinity was taking hold throughout Egypt and her territories.

THE NORTHWEST FRONTIER FORTS

Trouble was also brewing on the western edge of the Egyptian empire. At the beginning of the reign of Rameses II, traditional Libyan tactics—small warrior bands making lightning strikes into the Nile Valley—had caused only minor difficulties for the Egyptians. Now Libya had suffered a long period of drought, and whole populations of nomadic clans were marching east across the desert toward the Egyptian Nile Delta. These groups were made up of men, women, and children with all their worldly possessions, including herds of goat and cattle.

Another group called the sea peoples, who were made up of refugees from wars in Greece and Sardinia, as well as various pirates, were also looking for new places to live and threatening the Mediterranean coast from the sea.

Rameses decided that drastic action was needed. He set up a chain of fortresses stretching north from Memphis up along the western

Even in ruins, the remains of the temple of Karnak present an impressive sight.

edge of the Delta to the sea, and then out west along the coast toward Libya. The farthest of these fortresses was situated at Zawiyet Umm el-Rakham, which

is around 300 kilometers west of the city of Alexandria.

This fortress was situated at least one week's march from the edge of the western desert. It had square walls 150 meters long, 5 meters wide, and over 10 meters high, and one entrance on the north side protected by limestone towers. The walls enclosed what was effectively a small town, with temples, the palace of the commander (called Neb-Re), rows of storerooms, wells for fresh water, a village of small houses for the soldiers, workshops for making and mending weapons, kilns for making pottery, stables, and a chariot park.

Other goods such as olive oil, wine, and opium were imported from Crete, Greece, Cyprus, and Syria and show that the fort was also a center for trade with merchants who sailed south from Crete. However, the fortress would have been an unpleasant and frightening place to stay, as it was in the middle of nowhere and was called "the ends of the earth" by the Egyptians, and was surrounded by unfriendly Libyan tribesmen.

The other fortresses on the Mediterranean coast were probably similar in size. Some existing towns along the western edge of the Delta were now also turned into fortresses. Excavations at sites such as Tell Abqa'in have shown that these settlements were enclosed with the same high, thick, mud brick walls. Rameses made his mark at all these sites. In addition to covering the temple walls with paintings of himself, he even had his name carved on the inside of the new limestone wells constructed to give fresh water to the inhabitants.

Meanwhile, building work was continuing in other cities throughout Egypt. The new capital city at Piramesse was taking shape. Large temples, to Amen, Ra, Ptah, and Seth, were built at the corners of the city. The original summer palace of Seti stood in the center of the city, and Rameses greatly enlarged this building, adding halls, reception rooms,

Four large statues of Rameses guard the entrance to his temple at Abu Simbel.

bedroom suites, and gardens. He also built a vast hall in which to celebrate his first jubilee in year thirty (1249 BC). Many noblemen and government officials had large villas in the new city, and it was also home to thousands of craftsmen, soldiers, and

The Ramesseum, or memorial temple of Rameses, on the left bank of the Nile at Thebes

traders. The city soon became known through-out Egypt and beyond for the beauty of the new buildings. A letter from the scribe Pebes to his master Amenemope describes the new city:

> I have arrived at Piramesse, Beloved of Amen, and found it in extremely good con-dition . . . The residence is pleasant to live in; its countryside is full of everything good, and it has food and drink every day.

At Memphis, Rameses added halls to the main Ptah Temple and erected a series of colos-sal statues of himself that lined the entrance-way to the southern gate. He later boasted about this on a large *stela* erected in his temple at Abu Simbel. "I have enlarged thy house at Memphis, protected with everlasting works, with excellent labor, in stone wrought with gold and genuine costly stones."

At Thebes, the hypostyle hall at the Karnak Temple was finally finished and decorated. Rameses ordered that it should be opened for public worship, and he called it "The Place Where the Common People Extol the Name of His Majesty." The pylon gateway and courtyard at the Luxor Temple were also finished, and thirteen colossal statues of the king now stood in the new courtyard. There were also two seated and four standing statues of the king in front of the temple where all could see them. People passing by would have probably prayed to these and other statues of the king so that he might speak to the gods inside the temples on their behalf.

A limestone statue of Ramose, one of Rameses' royal scribes.

Work also continued on his memorial temple, the Ramesseum, on the west bank of the Nile. This temple was a mixture of traditional and new features. The most noticeable innovation was an enormous seated statue of the king in the first court, which is estimated to have weighed 1,000 tons. Inside the temple, the walls were decorated with traditional themes of the king and the gods, as well as matching processions of his sons and daughters.

A sandstone carving of a procession of priests

PEACE WITH THE HITTITES

After seven years on the Hittite throne, Mursill III was deposed by his more popular uncle Hattusilis. Now called Uri-Teshub, Mursill was sent into exile in Syria. Here he tried to stir up a rebellion against his uncle, and was promptly banished to Cyprus. From there he escaped to Egypt and the protection of Rameses II, where he continued his campaign against Hattusilis.

However, unfortunately for Uri-Teshub, Hattusilis was a very good negotiator. He sent a diplomat to Egypt carrying a letter from the emperor of the Hittites addressed to the pharaoh of Egypt. After many years of fighting, a peace treaty was finally agreed upon between them. This treaty was engraved on two huge silver tablets in a script called cuneiform. Excerpts from this treaty were also carved onto the

Guardian of the Doors or priest of the dead from the sarcophagus chamber, Tomb of Queen Nefertari, wife of Rameses II

walls of the Karnak Temple and the Ramesseum, and are also to be found on a clay tablet from the Hittite capital at Hattusas. The treaty included many interesting provisions in addition to a formal declaration of peace. The two kings agreed to stop fighting over Syrian territory and to form a defensive alliance against the Syrians. Political refugees and immigrants living across the border were extradited to their native countries.

An interesting provision at the end of the treaty outlines the humane treatment to be shown to the people affected by the extradition clauses: "Let not his house be injured, nor his wives, nor his children, let him not be killed, and let no injury be done to his ears, to his eyes, to his mouth, nor to his feet."

Both sides now celebrated the peace. Hattusil sent greetings to Rameses, and his wife Pudukhepa wrote to Queen Nefertari, and she wrote back, "With me your sister, all goes well; with my country all goes well. With you my sister, may all go well, with your country may all go well." After more good wishes, she ends the letter "Now I am in friendship and sisterly relations with my sister, the Great Queen, now and forever."

Friendship grew between the two countries. Correspondence continued between the two rulers. They sent each other many presents, including objects of gold and jewelry. The Egyptians, famous for their medical knowledge, also sent doctors to the Hittite royal family. In year thirty-three (1246 BC) Hattusil offered to send his daughter to marry Rameses. This marked the end of the wars of Rameses II, and for the rest of his reign Egypt was generally at peace with her neighbors.

FAMILY LIFE

Queen Nefertari was Rameses' favorite wife. She had at least ten children with him, including his eldest son Amenhirwonmef, his third son Prehirwonmef, and one of his favorite daughters, Meryetamen. Rameses' smaller temple at Abu Simbel was dedicated in part to Nefertari, and she and Meryetamen traveled with the king to the opening of the great temples at Abu Simbel in year twenty-four (1255 BC). Nefertari seems to have died soon after, and was buried in the Valley of the Queens on the west bank of the Nile at Thebes, where her tomb is one of the most beautiful in Egypt.

Iset Nofret next became the principal queen, but she also seems to have died soon after, although her tomb has not yet been found. Rameses now needed a new queen. Who could be a more suitable wife for a king of Egypt than the daughter

A limestone statue of Meryetamen, daughter and wife of Rameses II. It was quite common for Egyptian kings to marry their sisters and daughters.

of a king of Egypt? And so Rameses married his own daughter, Bint-Anath. He was later to marry three other daughters: Meryetamen, Nebettawi, and Hentmire.

Bint-Anath and Meryetamun shared the role of chief queen until year thirty-four, when they were joined by Hattusil's daughter. In autumn 1246 BC, the Hittite princess left the castle in the Hittite capital at Hattusas and traveled through Syria, Canaan, and the Sinai toward Egypt. She was accompanied by presents of animals, slaves, and precious jewels. Her mother came with her as far as Kadesh, where the group was met by Egyptian officials.

Finally, in February 1245 BC, she arrived at Piramesse to be welcomed by Rameses II. The whole county erupted in official celebration (paid for by the king) and a description of the marriage was carved on *stelae* in temples throughout Egypt.

Rameses decided to name his new queen Maathoreneferure, meaning "She who sees the Falcon [Rameses] who is the visible splendor of Ra." She lived in the royal palace for a while, and is written about in various inscriptions. However, her attraction seems to have paled quite quickly, and she was eventually packed off to live in the harem palace at Ghurob in the

An Egyptian official and his wife playing a board game. Note the pet cat under the wife's chair.

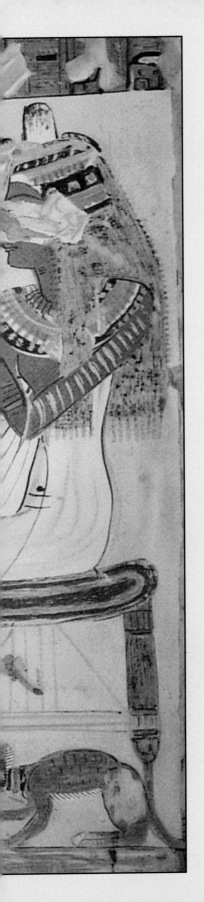

Faiyum. Ten years later another Hittite princess was sent to marry Rameses, but sadly neither her name nor what became of her is known.

Rameses had as many as 100 children. He outlived many of them, and between years twenty and thirty many of Rameses' sons died, including Amenhirkhopshef and Prehirwonmef. Prince Rameses was next heir to the throne, but he too died sometime between years twenty-five and fifty.

The next heir was Prince Khaemwaset. This prince had led a busy life as an important priest at Memphis. Khaemwaset was also very interested in the history and archaeology of Egypt. The Memphite necropolis is the site of most of Egypt's pyramids and temples dating from the Old and Middle Kingdoms. These ancient monuments had been neglected for many years,

A gold mask recovered from the wooden sar-cophagus of Rameses II

and many were now covered in sand or in ruins. Khaemwaset got permission from Rameses to restore these monuments, and also to label each pyramid with the correct name of the king buried inside.

The fifth heir was Rameses' thirteenth son, Merenptah, and it was he who eventually succeeded to the throne.

ROYAL JUBILEES

From the time of the earliest kings of Egypt, a special ritual had been performed to renew the king's powers. This was called the *heb-sed* or jubilee festival. In the New Kingdom, the first *heb-sed* was performed in the thirtieth year of the king's reign, and then every three years afterward. In year thirty, 1250 BC, Rameses' first jubilee was organized by Prince Khaemwaset in the specially built hall at Piramesse. This massive celebration lasted for two months, with all the high officials presented to the king, and with many ceremonies where the king was recrowned with the crowns of Upper and Lower Egypt. Religious services also took place in all the other temples in Egypt, and it was a time of mass celebration throughout the country.

A wall painting showing Rameses kneeling, flanked by the gods Anubis and Horus, from the sarcophagus chamber of Rameses' tomb.

Rameses reigned for so long that he went on to celebrate at least thirteen more jubilee festivals.

THE FINAL YEARS

The latter part of Rameses' reign passed without major incident. He was still active in his fifties and sixties, but he had outlived all of his friends and many of his wives and children, and was probably rather lonely in his later years.

In year sixty-six of his reign, at the age of eighty-nine or ninety, Rameses celebrated his fourteenth jubilee. He passed that winter in his palaces at Piramesse and Memphis. Medical evidence from his body shows that he suffered severe arthritis in his hips and hardening of the arteries in his lower legs, which would have made walking very painful. His teeth and gums were also badly decayed, and he probably had constant toothaches.

Wall paintings from the sarcophagus chamber of the tomb of Rameses II

CREDITS

EDITOR
Jake Goldberg

LAYOUT
Geri Giordano

SERIES DESIGN
Evelyn Horovicz

ABOUT THE AUTHOR

Susanna Thomas has a B.A. in Egyptian archaeology from University College, London, and was awarded a Ph.D. from Liverpool University in 2000. She has worked at sites all over Egypt, including in the Valley of the Kings, and runs excavations at Tell Abqa'in in the western Delta. She is currently a research fellow at Liverpool University and director of the Ramesside Fortress Town Project.

In the spring and summer of 1213 BC, Rameses stayed in his palace at Piramesse. Finally, in August of 1213 BC, Rameses died. During the next seventy days his body was carefully embalmed, and the new pharaoh Merenptah and his entourage accompanied the king's body as it sailed slowly up the river to Thebes. They disembarked on the west bank, and after conducting religious services in his temple, the Ramesseum, Rameses II was carried to the Valley of the Kings, where his body was finally laid to rest in his tomb.

Rameses II is a major figure in Egyptian history. He restored Egypt's power and glory throughout the ancient world, thereby completing what his grandfather and father had set out to do. He promoted many able men to run Egypt's vast bureaucratic government system, and he added many beautiful buildings to Egypt's cities. Indeed, Rameses built or added to more temples throughout Egypt and Nubia than any other pharaoh. His memory lived on throughout Egyptian history, and for the next 1,000 years he and his colossal statues were worshiped. Even today, his name and image live on, and he is remembered as Rameses the Great.

GLOSSARY

cultivation The season between September and April during which crops were planted and ripened.

dynasty Egyptian history was divided into thirty-one dynasties stretching from Menes in Dynasty One until the invasion of Alexander the Great in 332 BC. The reason for the change from one dynasty to the next is not always clear, but is usually associated with a change in the royal family or the location of the capital.

harvest The season between April and June when crops were harvested.

***heb-sed* festival** The ritual of royal regeneration, usually celebrated after thirty years of the king's reign but occasionally performed earlier.

Horus The sky-god, pictured with the head of a falcon, the son of the gods Osiris and Isis.

inundation The term used to describe both the event and the season of the annual flooding of Egypt, which took place between June and September.

ka The soul, or life force, of every ancient Egyptian.

Lower Egypt The northern half of the country stretching from Memphis to the Mediterranean coast.

Maat A goddess who embodied aspects of truth, justice, and harmony in the universe. The power of Maat regulated the seasons and the movement of the sun, the moon, and the stars. One of the main jobs of the king was to maintain the rule of Maat.

memorial temple A temple where the mortuary cult of the king was celebrated.

Memphis Capital city of ancient Egypt, close to modern-day Cairo. The city was known as Ineb-hedj, or "White Walls," and was the cult center of the god Ptah.

Nubia The region immediately south of Ancient Egypt; modern-day Sudan.

Osiris The god of the underworld. A deceased pharaoh would become Osiris.

pharaoh In the Old Kingdom the most common terms for the king were *hemef*, "His Majesty," or *nesw*, "King." From the New Kingdom onward the term pharaoh was used, which came from the name of the palace, which was *per-aa,* or "Great House."

Ramesseum The name of the memorial temple of Rameses II.

Upper Egypt The southern half of the country stretching from Memphis to Aswan.

Valley of the Kings The New Kingdom royal necropolis located on the west bank of the Nile, about three miles west of modern Luxor.

vizier The vizier or tjaty was the chief minister of the government. During the New Kingdom there were two viziers at Memphis and Thebes.

FOR MORE INFORMATION

ORGANIZATIONS
American Research Center in Egypt
United States Office
Emory University West Campus
1256 Briarcliff Road, NE
Building A, Suite 423W
Atlanta, GA 30332
(404) 712-9854
e-mail: arce@emory.edu

International Association of
   Egyptologists
United States Branch
Department of Ancient Egyptian,
   Nubian, and Far Eastern Art
Museum of Fine Arts
465 Huntington Avenue
Boston, MA 02115
Web site: http://www.mfa.org

JOURNALS
Ancient Egypt
Empire House
1 Newton Street
Manchester M1 1HW
England
e-mail: empire@globalnet.co.uk

WEB SITES

Due to the changing nature of Internet links, the Rosen Publishing Group, Inc., has developed an online list of Web sites related to the subject of this book. This site is updated regularly. Please use this link to access the list:

http://www.rosenlinks.com/lae/rama/

FOR FURTHER READING

Breasted, James. *Ancient Records of Egypt, Volume III: The Nineteenth Dynasty.* Chicago: University of Chicago Press, 2001.

Caminos, Ricardo. *Late Egyptian Miscellanies.* Oxford, England: Oxford University Press, 1954.

Kitchen, Kenneth A. *Ramesside Inscriptions, Translations, Volume II: Rameses II Royal Inscriptions.* Malden, MA: Blackwell, 1996.

Lichtheim, Miriam. *Ancient Egyptian Literature, Volume II: The New Kingdom.* Berkeley, CA: University of California Press, 1976.

Menu, Bernadette. *Ramses II, Greatest of the Pharaohs.* New York: Abrams, 1999.

Rees, Rosemary. *The Ancient Egyptians.* Woburn, MA: Butterworth-Heinemann, 1997.

Tiano, Oliver. *Ramses II and Thebes.* New York: Holt, 1995.

BIBLIOGRAPHY

Aldred, Cyril. *The Egyptians*. London: Thames & Hudson, 1998.

Baines, John, and Jaromir Malek. *Atlas of Ancient Egypt*. New York: Facts on File, 1993.

Davies, Vivian, and Renee Friedman. *Egypt Uncovered*. New York: Stewart, Tabori & Chang, 1998.

Freed, Rita. *Rameses II: The Great Pharaoh and His Time*. Denver, CO: Denver Museum of Natural History, 1987.

Hayes, William. *The Scepter of Egypt 2: The Hyksos Period and the New Kingdom*. New York: Metropolitan Museum of Art, 1990.

Kitchen, Kenneth A. *Pharaoh Triumphant: The Life and Times of Rameses II*. Warminster, England: Aris and Phillips, 1982.

Shaw, Ian, and Paul Nicolson. *British Museum Dictionary of Ancient Egypt*. London: British Museum Press, 1995.

Snape, Steven. *Egyptian Temples*. Princes Risborough, England: Shire, 1996.

INDEX

A massive sculpture of
the head of Rameses II